MW01245535

Joyful
Mess

A Joyful Mess

Devotions for
Surviving Early Motherhood

Evie Lynn Cunningham

TATE PUBLISHING
AND ENTERPRISES, LLC

Published by Tate Publishing & Enterprises, LLC
127 E. Trade Center Terrace | Mustang, Oklahoma 73064 USA
1.888.361.9473 | www.tatepublishing.com

Tate Publishing is committed to excellence in the publishing industry. The company reflects the philosophy established by the founders, based on Psalm 68:11,
"The Lord gave the word and great was the company of those who published it."

Book design copyright © 2015 by Tate Publishing, LLC. All rights reserved.
Cover design by Joseph Emnace
Interior design by Angelo Moralde

Published in the United States of America

ISBN: 978-1-68118-188-2
Family & Relationships / Parenting / General
15.03.06

Acknowledgments

First and foremost, I thank Jesus Christ for saving me from myself and from death in my sin. He has shown me the only way to life.

Thank you to my loving husband Bryan who believes in me and puts up with my messiness in every sense of the word. For his patience even when he's not. My life is meant to be spent with you, my love.

To my children who believe that anything is possible. You encourage me to be whatever I want to be. Ava, Lia, and Eli, without you, obviously I could never have written this devotional, as I would have no content. I love you guys!

To my parents and siblings, my in-laws and all the rest of my family that I hold so dear. You are my home, and I love you.

Also, to my many friends who listen to my stories and my jabbering on and on about this and that, and stick around anyway. You encourage me, and you help light up my days.

Lastly, to all you moms out there, who understand my mess because you live it too. I hope you enjoy this book. It was written from my heart to yours.

Contents

Introduction. 9

Nobody Warned Me 11

Ah, Motherhood 15

When I Grow Up 19

Beauty Down the Toilet. 23

Love Is Patient 27

The Naughty Word 31

Going to God in My Pretty Dress. 35

Little Girls and Belly Button Shirts 39

Am I a Bad Christian?. 41

Scene Three, Stage Right. 43

It's a Family Affair. 47

The Butterfly Incident 51

Livin' It Up in the Garbage Dump 55

A Lady and Her Mustache 59

Thou Shalt Not Swallow 63

Naughty or Nice 67

A Childish Panic. 71

Rest. 75

Love 77

Knees in the Gramble 81

Remember the Thorns 85

Distraction. 89

But Lord 93

Breakfast in Bed 97

Joy in the Jumble 101

Give Thanks. 105

Doing Dishes in Heaven 109

My BFF. 113

Nap Time 117

Encouragement and Pixie Hollow. 121

Of Babies and Missing Brain Cells 125

Finding My Worth in the Checkout Line. . . . 129

Introduction

For the last couple of years, I have had a sincere passion in my life to let other people know that they are not alone. I want moms to know that we all have struggles and life can be tough, but we are in this together. My hope for you is that you will somehow meet Jesus in these pages, and that you will grow closer to Him in the few minutes that you may have each day. He is for you, and so am I. Hang in there, momma. You've got this.

Nobody Warned Me

I am convinced. Babies should come with manuals. Or at least warning labels.

Warning: This child will be just like you. And not in the good way you were hoping for.

Warning: Baby may not sleep. Ever. And neither will you.

Warning: This child comes with frequent whining, eye rolling, stomping around, and slamming of doors. Punishment will be necessary, but difficult.

Warning: This child may do any of the following things on you: step, jump, sneeze, cough, spit, pee, vomit, poop, or fall asleep. Often two or more may occur at the same time.

Warning: This child is lacking in fear. He will jump off trampolines, fall out of shopping carts, swallow inappropriate objects, climb up ladders, get in the bathtub fully clothed, fall down stairs, fall out of bed, and get stuck underneath furniture. All before the age of fifteen months. You *will* grow more gray hairs.

Although you sort of have an idea of what you are getting in to, I believe we all have this naive belief that our kid won't be that bad. We think that life is going to be just hunky dory and each kid will be exactly the same, therefore, predictable. Oh, and they will all be angels, because we have this parenting thing all figured out.

People try to warn you, but you just ignore them. The warnings always come with a smile, or a laugh, or both along with a "You'll see."

Maybe that's because of the biggest warning label of all:

Warning: Although this child may be naughty, sick, frustrating, loud, unpredictable, fearless, whiny, annoying, cranky, and too energetic, they may also be overwhelmingly smart, cute, thoughtful, angelic, well mannered, sympathetic, beautiful little souls. And no matter what they may be at any given moment, the next it will change. You will be permanently attached to these creatures, and you will love them with a fierceness you have never experienced before. You will wear your heart on your sleeve and you will be a different person than you ever were without them. Your life will revolve around them for a season, and someday that season will pass and you will mourn its loss. It is recommended that you enjoy every moment while you can. Then when they come to have children of their own you can smile and laugh and say, "You'll see."

Thought for the Day

Is your life with kids what you expected? Maybe sometimes it's worse, but maybe sometimes it's better. When it does seem worse, make a list of all the great things that make parenthood a wonderful journey.

From God's Word

> Don't you see that children are God's best gift? The fruit of the womb his generous legacy? Like a warrior's fistful of arrows are the children of a vigorous youth. Oh, how blessed are you parents, with your quivers full of children! (Psalm 127:3–5a, The Message)

Prayer for Today

Heavenly Father, as much as I dreamed about what having children would be like, I was way off. It can be so hard, but so very, very wonderful. Show me how to raise them properly. Thank you so much for the blessing of my children. In your Son's Holy name. Amen.

Ah, Motherhood

Writer's block

I love to write down my thoughts, but sometimes it seems impossible. I get out my pen and paper, or try to type something out on the computer and nothing is there. It must be writer's block.

Okay, let's be honest. It's more like mother's block.

When I'm unable to write for a while, I miss it. But let's face it. I'm a mom. With a job. Two busy big kids. And a baby who doesn't sleep. Ever.

Okay, he sleeps. But not very well. Often, during my usual writing time, I'm either catching up on laundry or dishes or trying to put the little monster to bed. See, he has me figured out. He knows how to tug at my heart strings. He also knows how to annoy me enough to get his way. He does not go to bed on his own. He likes to take his bottle, pretend he's asleep, and then as soon as you move, he'll pop up with a big smile on his face and start to play. He'll wiggle around and talk and walk on the couch until he collapses in a strange position. Then his sister comes downstairs with some interesting reason to be out of bed. Tonight's was, "Mom, we are humid." Okay, I had to laugh at that one. But it wakes him up, and we have to start over from the beginning.

It's really pretty funny. Except when it isn't. Like at three in the morning when we do the whole routine again.

We try putting him in his crib. He doesn't cry. He screams. Nonstop. Tonight it was about an hour. But darnit I wasn't going to give in. The kid has to learn sometime. So does his momma. I have read somewhere that the French let their kids cry it out in their cribs at four months and they are well-rounded children.

I'm making an attempt at a well-rounded child.

Please don't think I'm complaining. I love my children with all my heart. My baby is a joy.

Except when he's not.

Life is hard sometimes. And sometimes we just have to roll with the punches and do our job as parents, spouses, and workers. I am determined to make this time special and enjoyable and important. My kids need me.

Besides, this phase will only last for such a short time. And someday, I'll miss it.

Thought for the Day

Does it sometimes feel like life is put on hold while you are raising your little babies? Do you miss the things you love, or feel like you have exchanged them for dirty diapers and arguing with little kids? Don't forget, motherhood is a dear and precious calling, and although it can be tough, each minute is so very important in the growth of your little ones. It won't be long and they will be all grown up.

From God's Word

> As a mother comforts her child, so will I comfort you; and you will be comforted over Jerusalem. (Isaiah 66:13, NIV)

Prayer for Today:

Lord, sometimes it feels like I have put my life on hold for my kids. It is so easy to forget that you have called me to raise these babies, and it is such an important job. As long as I keep my trust in you, I know that I can do this. I know that you hold both me and my children in your hands. Thank you for being there to guide me while I guide them. In Jesus' name. Amen.

When I Grow Up

A couple of days ago, Bryan and I watched a video about what you should do when you grow up. It made you think if money was no object, what would you want to do? In the video they say, whatever that thing is, you should do it.

So we asked Ava and Lia; what do you want to be when you grow up?

Ava wants to be a farm girl, an artist, and a number of other things. Lia wants to be a princess.

This week in Sunday school, we talked about fairy tales. It reminded me of my girls. When they are little, it is so simple for them to believe that they can grow up and be whatever they want. I want them to keep on believing that. But I also don't want them to become disillusioned with the fact that sometimes in this world it seems the dragon is impossible to slay, the prince may not be so charming, and the glass slipper may go to someone else.

What I can teach them is that they *can* grow up to be the princess.

How?

Jesus.

They have the opportunity to be adopted into the kingdom of God and be daughters of the King of kings and Lord of lords. And if they choose this, they can be more than they ever possibly imagined.

They may have to live with the dwarves for a while. They may feel like they are being chased by the wicked witch. They may have to face a few giants. But if they stick with God, He will stick with them and fight the bad guys every time.

If they follow the will of the Lord and ask for his dreams to become theirs, they will live happily ever after—both here and eternally in heaven.

It's a truth that I am learning myself now. And I have decided when I grow up, I am going to be a princess, too.

Thought for the Day

When you were little, what did you want to be when you grew up? What do your kids want to be? If you have not become what you want to be, don't give up! God can see you through to the finish.

From God's Word

> Instead, speaking the truth in love, we will in all things grow up into him who is the Head, that is, Christ. (Ephesians 4:15, NIV, 1984)

Prayer for Today

Jesus, when I was little, I wanted to be so many things. Some of them I became, some I did not. Some of the things I am still working on. The thing is, with you, I know I will grow up to become exactly what I am meant to be. Thank you for guiding my steps and being my King. In your name. Amen.

Beauty Down the Toilet

Two and a half years ago, I gave birth to a bouncing baby boy and was blessed with a family of two beautiful girls and this handsome little man-child. And a body that I would quickly exchange if I could. Needless to say, right after he was born, not a lot of my garments were really doing me many favors in the looks category, if they fit at all. Being that I had a job that required me to look presentable, I had been in search of some nice clothes to make me look beautiful. My cheap self loves clearance racks! Anyway, after maternity leave ended, I went back to work, adorned in my sassy new clothes. I was pulling off a look that I couldn't deny was fabulous! I felt prettier than I had in a long time and my pride welled up just a bit.

Four o'clock rolled around one day and I took a break to pump. But first, I had to go to the potty (as we moms of little ones call it). So I sat down, did my business, and realized that my beautiful new skirt had found itself in the toilet. Yes. It's true. And I had peed on it. At work.

Excellent.

So, I thought, *now what*? I still have half an hour left of work to get through, and I certainly can't pull off the leggings I had been wearing underneath. I am a hefty girl. Leggings for me are only permissible under a big fancy skirt. I did the only thing I could do. I laughed. A lot. I took off my skirt, stuck it in the sink, and washed it out. Then I hung it on the door of the bathroom and did what I came to do. Then I dried it off the best I could, put it back on, and went back to work—with a wet skirt. All the while thinking, pride always comes before the fall.

Friends, this is life. Stuff happens over which we have no control. Sometimes it is terrible, heartbreaking, and life changing. Sometimes it's just pee on your skirt. But there are lessons in all of these things, and we can learn so much by carrying His Word in our hearts for the big things and the little. I was reminded today that my clothes don't matter. I am beautiful in my skin in any clothes, and my God cares for me. He gave us the ability to laugh at ourselves, and He is with us when we react with laughter or with tears. He is a wonderful Lord—what a friend we have in Jesus!

Thought for the Day

Do you have any embarrassing moments like this? What did you do with them? When something embarrassing happens, use your God-given sense of humor. Laugh!

From God's Word

> "All this time and money wasted on fashion—do you think it makes that much difference? Instead of looking at the fashions, walk out into the fields and look at the wildflowers. They never primp or shop, but have you ever seen color and design quite like it? The ten best-dressed men and women in the country look shabby alongside them. If God gives such attention to the appearance of wildflowers—most of which are never even seen—don't you think he'll attend to you, take pride in you, do his best for you?" (Matthew 6:28–30, The Message)

Prayer for Today

Lord, I sometimes take more stock in my appearance than I should, and worry about what I look like more than I put my trust in you. When this happens, thank you for reminding me what is most important. Thank you for the sense of humor you gave us as your people to take in the embarrassing moments and the hard parts of life. You are so good. In Jesus' name. Amen.

Love Is Patient

Sometimes, when I have been doing a lot of "Christiany" things, I have the tendency to think, "Boy, I'm being a pretty good Christian." I begin to get a big head and think I am extra holy and great.

Then there are days like this:

I had zero patience for my beautiful children. They were doing what kids do. Eli cried a lot. The girls were getting along, but that comes with an inability to accomplish the task at hand. Ava had homework that she really wasn't interested in figuring out, and to be honest, I wasn't really interested in helping her. Frustration grew and when we were half an hour past bedtime, and not yet in bed, I had to resist the urge to yell and scream.

I was pretty short with them when I tucked them in. We still said prayers and gave hugs, but I had had it with the dillydallying and it was bedtime. Good night.

However, once I had calmed down a bit and had an opportunity to think, I quickly felt the guilt come on. I had not treated them badly, but I certainly had no patience with them. They were just kids being kids. They didn't move as quickly as I wanted them to, but they were getting along for the most part. They didn't accomplish the tasks I wanted them to accomplish, but I am the parent, and I didn't give them the structure to do so. I expect them to act like adults sometimes and that isn't fair. It is my job to lay down the foundation, teach them, and help them along as they learn. They must be held accountable, but I must be patient while they figure it out.

Funny, but it seems to me that I don't meet expectations laid out for me in the Bible either (nor do I meet expectations laid out for me by other people). But God doesn't scream and yell. He is ever patient with me. I screw up all the time. But He just holds me as His child and lets me learn as I go. He speaks to me lovingly and waits while I get it all figured out. I am held accountable, but He never loses His temper.

I think I have a lot to learn about parenting from my Heavenly Father. Good thing He is patient while I get there.

Thought for the Day

Do you ever begin to think you are doing a great job at life, then something happens to humble you, like it did (and does) to me? What will you do when this happens? Try talking to God about it. Know He forgives you, so you can certainly forgive yourself.

From God's Word

> The Lord is not slow in keeping his promise, as some understand slowness. Instead he is patient with you, not wanting anyone to perish, but everyone to come to repentance. (2 Peter 3:9, NIV)

> So then, dear friends, since you are looking forward to this, make every effort to be found spotless, blameless, and at peace with him. (2 Peter 3:14, NIV)

Prayer for Today

Lord, sometimes I think I am already a good person and don't need you. Then I am reminded that I am imperfect and messy, and in desperate need of a patient, loving God such as you. Thank you for having the patience with me that I don't always have. Please make me more like you so I can be a good parent to my children. Thank you. In your name. Amen.

The Naughty Word

I was bringing my middle child, Lia, to preschool one day when she piped up from the backseat.

"Mom, the other day, Gabby said a naughty word. It was the naughtiest one of all, but I don't want to tell you what it is."

This ought to be interesting, I thought.

"Do you want me to tell you, Mom? I don't really want to."

"Then don't tell me, Lia."

"Well, I don't really want to, Mom. But I will if you want me to…I really think that maybe I should. 'Cuz it's the naughtiest one of all and Gabby shouldn't be saying it."

"Okay then, you can tell me if you want to," I replied. "If you don't want to say it out loud, just whisper it to me later."

When we got to school, I was a little nervous about what she was going to tell me. To be quite honest, I was prepared to hear something nasty come out of her little innocent mouth.

I opened the car door and leaned in close. She whispered quietly, "Gabby said, 'Oh…my….god!'" Her eyes grew wide as she waited for my reaction. "That is the very worst word of all."

My first reaction was relief that the word I was expecting didn't come out of her mouth. I was also so very proud that she understood that our family does not take the Lord's name in vain. But mostly, I was disappointed in myself that it didn't occur to me that that might be the naughtiest word of all. Using the Lord's name that way makes me cringe, but I have grown used to hearing it, and occasionally, using it myself.

Her little girl's wisdom reminded me of something very important. God's name is not to be taken lightly but instead to be revered.

Thought for the Day

Do you ever find yourself taking God's name lightly, or using Jesus's name in ways you should not? Does it bother you when you hear others do this? Practice using God's name only in reverence to Him, and when you hear His name used, use that moment to worship who He truly is.

From God's Word:

> "You shall not misuse the name of the Lord your God, for the Lord will not hold anyone guiltless who misuses his name. (Deuteronomy 5:11, NIV)

Prayer for Today

Lord, so often when I hear your name used improperly, I don't even think twice. At times, I misuse your name myself as well, and that saddens me. Please help me to remember that your name is holy, and worthy of only praise from my lips. Help me to teach my children this truth as well. You are a good God, and your name is so very precious to me. I thank you for allowing me to speak to you and to pray in your name and in the name of your son Jesus. Praise be to you, Lord. Amen

Going to God in My Pretty Dress

A few years ago, I was on my way to a local Christian mom's group for our monthly meeting. At that time, I held the position of a leader in the group. I did not feel like much of a leader, but more like a fraud.

I had allowed the stress of work and motherhood to consume me, and rather than go to God for rest, I went to other people, things, and nasty habits. I had quit praying to God for fear that He would be uninterested in what I had to say. I had strayed too far and allowed my spiritual life and relationship with the Lord to become almost nonexistent.

As I neared the church, my eldest daughter piped up out of her long silence from her car seat in the back, "Mom, you have to wear a special dress to talk to God."

I was a little taken aback. "No, you don't! Who told you that?" I replied.

"Nobody…I just know."

I quickly explained that her idea was simply not true. You did not have to wear anything special to go to God. To speak to Him did not require a special dress code.

She lit up, very pleased with my response. "You mean I can go to Him just the way I am?!" she asked.

"Of course!"

At that moment, my little student became my teacher. I was reminded that you did not, in fact, need to be "dressed up special" to talk to God. He takes us just as we are.

Thought for the Day

How often do you choose something other than God to go to with your troubles, stress, or even thankfulness, because you are afraid He is uninterested? Do you feel that you have to have it all together to be acceptable to Him? Whatever may be going on, know that you can go to Him.

From God's Word

> Therefore, since we have a great high priest who has ascended into heaven, Jesus the Son of God, let us hold firmly to the faith we profess. For we do not have a high priest who is unable to empathize with our weaknesses, but we have one who has been tempted in every way, just as we are—yet he did not sin. Let us then approach God's throne of grace with confidence, so that we may receive mercy and find grace to help us in our time of need. (Hebrews 4:14–16, NIV)

Prayer for Today

Thank you for the precious reminder, dear Lord, that I may come to you in whatever mess I may be in. You do not require a special dress, or a spotless life for us to approach you. Your Son gave His spotless life in our place, that through Him, we have a direct line straight to you, our King. In His name. Amen.

Little Girls and Belly Button Shirts

My girls and I were watching TV one day as some scantily clad women danced across the screen. Different thoughts flooded my mind all at once.

How do I explain to my girls that we shouldn't dress that way?

Maybe we need to get rid of the TV.

Is that what men like? More importantly, is that what my husband likes?

But the loudest thought of all was, I look *nothing* like that.

Suddenly, my seven-year-old spoke up.

"Mom, you would look really good in a shirt that shows your belly button."

Ah, the blessed innocence of little children.

I quickly let her know that I would *not* be wearing such a shirt, nor would she. In little girl language, I explained the value of modesty.

And then, with a big smile (on my face and in my heart), I thanked her for the wonderful compliment.

Thought for the Day

Do you ever look at the women on TV and in magazines and compare yourself to them? What can you do to have confidence in your own special beauty? Remember who you belong to.

From God's Word

> Charm is deceptive, and beauty is fleeting; but a woman who fears the Lord is to be praised. (Proverbs 31:30, NIV)

Prayer for Today

Lord, you know the self-condemning thoughts that enter my mind when I see beautiful people on TV and plastered across magazine covers in the grocery store. Help me understand where my true beauty comes from, no matter what my outside package looks like. Help me raise my children to see true beauty as well and to strive toward that in their lives as I wish to on my own. Thank you so much for the loving way you have made me. In your precious name. Amen.

Am I a Bad Christian?

Sometimes I feel I will never be what God wants me to be. I feel like a bad Christian who never reads the Bible, only prays before dinner (if that) and hasn't made it to church on time in months. My time is spent wiping noses and butts, chauffeuring kids, working at my paying job, keeping the baby out of the dog dish, ushering kids out the door and back in the door, in the tub, out for play, to school, to church, to birthday parties, to bed. And oh yes, I have to get us all fed and squeeze my own shower in there somewhere.

I try to teach my kids about God, and goodness, and tithing, and I get comments like this:

"But, Mom, I am giving! I am giving unto the cashier!"

In the midst of everything, I often barely have time to think, let alone sit down, read the Bible, and talk to God. But on the days that I do take a minute to sit down, have a conversation with Him, and open up my Bible to take in some life-giving words, it is oh so worth it.

Somehow, I seem to have more time, and it seems to be well spent. My attitude is better, and my life seems important.

My responsibilities don't change. My kids don't mind better; my life doesn't get easier, but it's restored. More worth it. I become more thankful for the chaos.

Thought for the Day

Do you sometimes feel like a bad Christian? Like maybe God doesn't like you anymore because you aren't doing a very good job? Remember, it is important that through your faith you do good deeds as well, but I have some good news for you…It's not about you. Jesus died so we don't have to do, we just have to follow Him and the good will be obvious.

From God's Word

> I know your deeds. See, I have placed before you an open door that no one can shut. I know that you have little strength, yet you have kept my word and have not denied my name. (Revelation 3:8, NIV)

Prayer for Today

Lord, I, on my own, am certainly not worthy of your love or grace, and yet you patiently pursue me anyway. Because of your precious Son, I am allowed to be in your presence no matter the mess I am in. All I can say is thank you. There is no other God but you.

In the precious name of Jesus. Amen.

Scene Three, Stage Right

When you have kids, each stage has a point that feels like it will never end. The nine months of pregnancy can feel endless and miserable. The baby stages are full of dirty diapers and sleepless nights, walking around like a zombie smelling like baby puke. The toddler years are spent chasing kids around using the word "no!" 574 times a day, taking things away that the stinkers can't have. The elementary years seem to be spent with the kids now believing that their teacher is smarter than you, and your new most used words are "Hurry up!" As for the teenage years, I can only imagine.

Along with seeing all of the messy stuff, I can look back and see all of the wonderful things through each stage too. With the babies, the snuggling and yummy clean baby smell. The toddlers, their personalities forming and coming out, all the new words they learn and their little giggles. The school years, watching them learn to read and write and begin to discover their talents.

In each and every stage, if we try to watch very closely, I think God gives us daily gifts through our children. He gave us these lovelies to raise as our own and teach them and nurture them to the best of our abilities. They are ours for a reason. My three little ones are meant to have me as their mother and my husband as their father. We will mess up, we will get frustrated, and tired and overwhelmed. But through it all, with God's help, we will love and enjoy and shape these little gems. Someday, we will see what God made them to be, and be grateful that all the while He allowed us to help.

Thought for the Day

Most moms have those moments when they wonder if the stage they are in will ever end. They feel frustrated and tired. Are you there? When you are, remember to take note of all the awesome things you are experiencing at the same time. When you look back, these are the times you may miss.

From God's Word

> There is a time for everything, and a season for every activity under the heavens:. (Ecclesiastes 3:1, NIV)

Prayer for Today

Lord, sometimes my days seem endless and frustrating. I wonder if I am doing any good in the stage I am in right now. But then you remind me of the good with some wonderful new experience with my children. Thank you for allowing me to experience this, and to guide them through their lives. In your precious name. Amen.

It's a Family Affair

I come from a background of blended families. I lived in some very different circumstances before I finally settled into what I now call my family when speaking of my childhood. I lived with my dad, stepmom, and my three siblings. Because my childhood was very different than that of my children's, sometimes I am in a situation where I need to explain to my kids my childhood's family dynamics.

There came one particular day that my kids were having a lot of trouble understanding how all of my family was related. They have many grandparents and great-grandparents. Their little brains couldn't seem to get it all sorted out on who was who, and why I had more than just two parents. My kids are blessed to have my husband and I still happily married as their parents, so they just weren't understanding the concept of stepparents.

Being that I spent much of my years with my dad and stepmom, and they have a very close relationship with their Nana (my stepmother), we have had a lot of discussions regarding that particular situation. Without trying to confuse them too much, or get into more variables than their little brains needed to know, each time this was brought up, I did the very best I could explaining how I grew up.

During this particular discussion, after all was said and done, my kids sat with confused looks on their faces. Until suddenly, my little girl's eyes got wide and she exclaimed, "Hey! This is no fair! I want a stepmom!"

What can one possibly say to that?

Thought for the Day

What kind of family did you grow up in? Are your children growing up in a similar situation, or is it very different? Whatever your family dynamics, don't forget to remind your kids that you love them very much, and that they have a Father in heaven who loves them too.

From God's Word

> For whoever does the will of my Father in heaven is my brother and sister and mother. (Matthew 12:50, NIV)

Prayer for Today

God, my family situation was so different than that of my children's, and the older they get, the more situations they will see that don't always make sense, and aren't always what you had in mind for a family. However, if we choose to follow you, we become part of your family. Thank you for giving me the earthly family you have, and thank you for making me a part of your family, too. In Jesus' name. Amen.

The Butterfly Incident

Shortly after my little family moved into our first real house, we quickly learned that owning a house wasn't all it was cracked up to be. We were very happy with our humble little abode, but we were sharing our home with some less than desirable creatures. I was killing big ugly bugs on a regular basis. A big colony of ants had moved into our front entry ceiling. And, we were killing wasps inside the kitchen more than I would like to admit. But worst of all, we had bats. Lots of them.

We thought that the bats were contained at the peak of the roof, and we had ruled out the existence of them in the attic. The sound of their little scratches was off-putting, but we lived with it, and they seemed harmless enough.

However, at about 1:00 a.m. one morning, my eldest, Ava, came running into my bedroom, followed by her sister.

"Mom, there is a butterfly in my room, and it just landed right next to my face on my pillow!"

Hmmm, a butterfly, huh. I groggily rolled over and slowly crawled out of my bed, mumbling that I would take care of it. I armed myself with a wad of toilet paper to take care of what I was hoping would just be a big moth.

Something swooped quickly over my head back and forth across the room and landed on the curtain. It was a big, ugly bat. Okay, it was a little ugly bat, but it seemed as though I was facing Godzilla.

I followed the example of my daughter and ran down the stairs into my bedroom where my whole family was waiting and then I woke my husband.

"Honey, it's not a butterfly, it's a bat. You need to go kill it. Please. Now!'"

My poor husband went upstairs armed with a tennis racket and a plastic bag. The girls and I listened carefully on the baby monitor for any signs that our brave knight had slain the beast.

Not long after, he came back downstairs. No luck. He moved to the couch to finish his night of sleeping peacefully, while the girls and I snuggled under blankets. I told them it would be all right, and that they should just pray. They slept soundly after that while I listened to the bat swoop back and forth across their bedroom, eyes wide and thoughts filled with anxiety. It wasn't until closer to 4:00 a.m. that my brave husband finally won the battle.

My daughters slept soundly because I had them pray. They had me and their dad to protect them, and God to seal the deal. I had God too, but instead of praying myself, I just told my daughters to do so.

The next morning, I realized my mistake. I was reminded that even bats were created by God, and he is in control of all. All I need to do is pray for peace, and he will do the rest.

Thought for the Day

Do you ever give your children good advice and teach them the right thing to do, but do the opposite yourself? Remember that God holds you in his hands, and the best place to go is always with Him. Prayer is good in all circumstances.

From God's Word

> So do not fear, for I am with you; do not be dismayed, for I am your God. I will strengthen you and help you; I will uphold you with my righteous right hand. (Isaiah 41:10, NIV)

Prayer for Today

Lord, although you tell us so many times in your Word not to fear, I still fear even the smallest of things. Help me to always go to you with my fear, whether it be huge life-changing circumstances, or little ugly bats. Thank you for always holding me together in your hand. In Jesus' name. Amen.

Livin' It Up in the Garbage Dump

Every day I get where I need to go in a beaten up garbage truck.

Okay, so it's actually a minivan full of trash.

On the outside, it's really quite nice. Oh, there are a few dents here and a few scratches there, but it's not too shabby. But on the inside, it is stained with spilt sodas and remnants of quickly snarfed down lunches on the go. It is full of old homework and birthday party invitations. There are candy wrappers, melted crayons, broken toys, and pieces of fallen out doll hair. There are mismatched mittens, hats, and some sweatshirts. I think the chicken nuggets my daughter didn't eat last month are still in there.

Under the hood and under the van aren't much better. It is in need of many parts, which make the van squeal and whir with loud unpleasant noises. There is no heat in the winter and no air in the summer. The driver's window doesn't work, and until I recently replaced the battery, there was no guarantee that when I shut it off it would turn back on.

Needless to say, because of neglect and lack of work (and funds), the van looks pretty good on the outside, but it's really quite awful on the inside.

I can easily get like that, too. I often neglect my inside in so many ways. I don't eat right or exercise and I get sick. I don't get enough sleep, and I don't function like I should. I don't take time for me and I get snappy with others. I watch TV shows that I shouldn't and fill my mind with garbage that doesn't come out as easily as it should. But most importantly, when I don't spend time with the One who created me, I really get full of garbage. When I don't spend the time in the Word, or praying, I can get cranky, run down, depressed, and nasty. I look messy and ugly on the inside, no matter what I look like on the outside. I need to make time every day to clean out my insides by filling them with goodness.

Thought for the Day

Has it ever occurred to you how easy it is to fill your mind and body with garbage, and how hard it is to get it out? Make a goal to spend some time with the Lord each day to keep your insides squeaky clean.

From God's Word

> All of us have become like one who is unclean, and all our righteous acts are like filthy rags; we all shrivel up like a leaf, and like the wind our sins sweep us away.
>
> Yet you, Lord, are our Father. We are the clay, you are the potter; we are all the work of your hand. (Isaiah 64:6, 8, NIV)

Prayer for Today

Lord, how very easy it is to get full of garbage. When I make bad choices in what I fill my mind and body with, goodness has a much harder time of showing itself. But when I choose to come to you, I can be clean and tidy on the inside where it really counts. Help me to remember the importance of choosing you each day so your light shines through me, no matter my outside cover. In your name. Amen.

A Lady and Her Mustache

When we become moms, especially with multiple children, our once important beauty routines go right out the window. We have no time, or want for that matter, to pause in front of a mirror to actually look at ourselves. We tend to forget that others can still see what we look like, and when it does occur to us, it can be quite embarrassing.

My realization hit one day at a birthday party. We were enjoying our time when Ava climbed up on my lap. We were snuggling and giggling and making silly faces when she ran her finger across my upper lip and loudly declared to the world, "Mom! You have a mustache!"

It seemed the party came to a dead halt as everyone turned and looked at me to await my reaction.

"Yes, honey, God made everyone with a little hair above their lip."

"Even girls?"

"Yep, even girls."

"But, Mom, yours is really black and long. I think you need to shave."

Sigh.

This was a kind reminder that I had been neglecting myself. I was really glad she didn't notice my few long chin hairs and caterpillar brows while she was examining my face. Oh well, I was already married, and not looking for a date.

Come to think of it, my husband thought it was hilarious. At least he and I both know that the mustache on my face is no indication of the softness in my heart.

Thought for the Day

Have your once important beauty routines gone out the window since having kids? Or do you take the time to beautify yourself? If you don't already, take time once in a while to care for your own looks, and take the time to feel great, but be careful to remember, your beauty does not come from the outside.

From God's Word

> The king is enthralled by your beauty; honor him,
> for he is your lord. (Psalm 45:11, NIV, 1984)

Prayer for Today

Father, in the hustle and bustle of my daily life, I often completely forget to care for myself in ways that I should. Help me to remember, however, that my beauty comes not from the outside, but from within. You are enthralled with my beauty because of my love for you and for your Son. Thank you for seeing the true beauty within. In your holy name. Amen.

Thou Shalt Not Swallow

All kids are born with the uncanny ability to somehow swallow things they shouldn't. With my eldest, it was a dime I had to faithfully search for in her diaper for a week. My middle, a broken ring pop that cut off her airway momentarily until her little body expelled it. But my third, he takes the cake.

He was crawling around on the floor at just over a year old, when suddenly he began to choke on something. We gave him a little slap on the back and the something slid down his throat. All was well, but being the "better safe than sorry" type, I took him to the doctor anyway. The doctor and I joked about how I would likely be searching in another diaper. Then the x-rays came back.

My tiny little tot had swallowed a two-inch sewing needle, and it had rested right in his little stomach. The doctor's demeanor turned quickly from easygoing to slightly panicked as she made some phone calls to get us into a local major hospital for evaluation as to the next course of action. This needle would not be coming out on its own.

We put out a call for prayer.

The surgeons at the hospital determined that they would have to attempt removal by pulling the needle back out through his throat, but we had to be prepared for more invasive and dangerous surgery. My husband and I were all nerves while the little stinker was completely oblivious to the risks ahead and was as happy and rambunctious as ever.

Ten hours, two ERs, four x-rays, and multiple medical personnel later, I was chasing my completely healthy, unscathed little angel down a dark hospital corridor trying to quiet his laughter so patients could sleep. We drove the hour home and back to life as usual. I truly believe that only by God's grace did things end up the way they did. It was a special miracle, just for us.

Thought for the Day

Has one of your kids ever gotten into a dangerous situation that only God could fix? If that ever happens, reach out in prayer. God hears the prayers of His people. Remember that miracles do happen.

From God's Word

> You are the God who performs miracles; you display your power among the peoples. (Psalm 77:14, NIV)

Prayer for Today

God, sometimes things happen to my kids that are scary and get me all in a tizzy. But you, Lord, can still work miracles when you choose, and sometimes you choose to work them for me. Help me to remember next time that if something scary happens to my children, the best place to go is to you in prayer. Thank you for hearing me. In Jesus' name. Amen.

Naughty or Nice

I was on my way to work one day when a man gave me the naughty finger.

He didn't just stick it up at me. He violently shook his fist with a vengeance, face distorted and finger up in a flare.

He was obviously angry. I had cut him off in traffic. It was an honest mistake. He had his turn signal on and was driving slowly, so I turned out. As it was, he wasn't actually turning so I inadvertently cut him off. Thank goodness no one got hurt.

But actually I did get hurt. My feelings were hurt. My ego was hurt. My calm demeanor was hurt. My happiness was shoved.

I would like to say that I brushed it off and moved on. But that would be dishonest.

Here's what really happened:

He forcefully shoved that naughty finger out at me and I lost my cool. Road rage took over. I sat in my car and screamed out how it was his fault because his turn signal was on. I was so disgusted by his actions that I was bound to hurt him back.

Here's the thing—no one was affected but me. He couldn't hear me. We were in our vehicles with the windows up, driving in opposite directions. My reaction would have no effect on him, I'm sure. But the rest of my day was rough. I went back to work with angry tears running down my face. I sniffled for a bit in my cubicle and had to explain to my coworker what was wrong. I passed on my distress at this rudeness to her. And others the next day. Then my attitude passed to my children at home.

At the time, I thought, well, this guy was a jerk! How dare he act that way! What if my children had been in the car? Had he never accidentally cut someone off? I certainly hadn't done it on purpose, but he felt the need to show me how he felt. And for goodness' sake, I wanted others to agree with me! He was wrong and I was right. Right?

Then came the conviction. The Holy Spirit had been whispering to me the whole time, and I didn't want to listen at first. My reaction to this man's anger was just as bad. Maybe not to other people, but to God. The anger that burned in me was not a righteous anger. It was sinful. My complaining and "holier than the naughty finger guy" attitude was wrong. I affected other people's happiness because I wanted my story told.

Let me just say, I don't think people should act the way that this person did. I will probably always be sensitive to reactions like that. But it's time to admit that my actions are no better. It's time to pray for those people, and to admit my own selfishness and sinfulness, and let God handle the rest. I can't be a good example to my children when I stoop down to the level of wrongdoing. If there is a next time, I hope I do better.

Thought for the Day

Do you tend to carry on your bad moments when you are treated wrongly? Do you pass on your attitude to others? Think of how your children see you when this happens, and strive to treat others the way you want to be treated.

From God's Word

> Do not seek revenge or bear a grudge against any-one among your people, but love your neighbor as yourself. I am the Lord. (Leviticus 19:18, NIV)

Prayer for Today

Lord, when someone mistreats me, it is so very hard not to want revenge, or at least to tell everyone about what happened. I know when I do this, it hurts you. Help me to remember that you see everything, and you will take care of things according to your good timing. Thank you for being all powerful and all loving. In Jesus' name. Amen.

A Childish Panic

I was in the shower one day when I heard a panicked cry come from the other room.

"Mom!"

It was a banter between myself in the noisy shower and my panicked four-year-old trying to tell me something. I was a little concerned. I finally convinced her that I couldn't hear her and she needed to come in and speak loudly so I could understand the problem.

"Someone put a money sticker on my picture! Now someone is going to buy it!"

I tried not to giggle out loud as I calmly explained to her that no one was going to buy her drawing. She could not be consoled as she was sure that someone was going to buy that drawing because someone else had put a money sticker on it. She wanted to know who did it and why they would do such a thing.

I kept my cool, relieved that I could hide my amusement. I finally convinced her that no one was going to come into our house and buy her picture just because there was a price tag on it.

As I got dressed, it occurred to me, how often do I panic about something and quickly run to God in a tizzy about who did what and why and how I should handle it? I imagine Him trying to contain His amusement at my unnecessary reaction. To me, these situations seem big and out of control. To Him, they are childish worries of no concern at all.

Because my child finally listened to me, I was able to calm her worries and send her on her way. We, as adults, have the experience to know that if we only listen to our Heavenly Father, He can calm our worries as well. We are His children and He cares for us.

I pray that next time, I remember that my worries are nothing to a King who can do all.

Thought for the Day

How many times have you panicked and run to God in worried prayer over something silly? Remember next time you do this, you've gone to the right place!

From God's Word

> Can any one of you by worrying add a single hour to your life? (Matthew 6:27, NIV)

Prayer for Today

Lord, I know that sometimes I worry about the silliest of things. Thank you for listening to my prayers even in these moments and helping me to remember that there is no need for me to worry in any circumstance, big or small. You are truly the One who can calm my fears. In your name. Amen.

Rest

It was almost midnight and rather than being tucked away in my nice warm bed, I was standing in the baby's room and both of us were crying. Loudly.

He put me over the edge.

The whole night was a rough one. I had a to-do list a mile long. Okay, so it was really just a cloud of thoughts in my head. Anyway, I had so many things to do, and instead, I held the baby for two hours trying to get him to sleep. I finally got him down, started one of my projects, got ready for bed, and he woke back up. All I could do was cry as I thought of all the things I had left unfinished. And all the sleep I wouldn't be getting.

It's so easy in the midst of the mess I live in to become overwhelmed. In fact, I often do become just that. Completely. Over. Whelmed.

But then, tucked away in the back of my mind is the verse in Matthew where Jesus tells me to come to him. He knows I'm weary. He knows I'm burdened. But he offers me rest. If I just take that minute that I don't think I have and seek Him out, I find the rest that I so badly need. Rather than being overwhelmed, I find peace. I find comfort. I find my burdens lifted and my soul renewed. I find the grace to get through another sleepless night, another unfinished to-do list, another normal day.

Rest. Who doesn't love that?

Thought for the Day

When raising children, it is so easy to become burdened and weary with all the daily activities we have. Do you find that you forget that God offers you rest? Go to Him and receive what he offers you.

From God's Word

> Come to me, all you who are weary and burdened, and I will give you rest. (Matthew 11:28, NIV)

Prayer for Today

Lord, I am often weary and burdened with all of the daily activities that my life requires of me. When I forget to come to you, I don't receive the rest that I need. Thank you for the reminder that I can come to you and lay down all of my burdens, those light and heavy, and receive rest from you. In Jesus' name. Amen.

Love

Love.

What does that even mean?

I love chocolate. I love a good book. I love when the sun shines down on my face and a slight breeze passes by. I love the warmth of my blankets and the comfort of my bed after a hard day.

But love must be deeper than that…

I love my kids with the fierceness of a mama bear. I love my friends and family. I love my husband so much it almost hurts. Sometimes this love does hurt. It can be fickle.

True love is a verb. It is not an emotion, but an action. Love is a choice that is sometimes very hard to make. To love is to bend your will to do for others when they don't necessarily deserve it.

But more than that even…

Love is to set aside your own desires. It is to place something higher than yourself. It is to deny yourself and your selfish ambitions.

God tells us we must love Him with all of our heart, soul, and strength.

I must take my heart and hand it over to Him. I must place in his hands my kids, my family, my husband. All that I hold so close I must choose to let go into his arms.

I must take all of my soul and hand it over to Him. My talents, my desires, my dreams. All that I have ever wanted must be sacrificed on the altar for God. I must give Him my goals and trust that He will take care of it. I must trust that He will give me the gift of His will and His grace when I do this.

I must take all the strength in my body and mind and hand it over to Him. All that I think holds me together needs to be given up. Everything I believe I have that makes me strong must be placed in His hands. My knowledge, my experiences, my strengths. My body itself must be given back to Him. For where I am weak, He can be strong.

All of this sometimes seems so overwhelming. It goes against every grain I have in my body to give it all up. I want to hold close. He wants me to let go.

This is not easy. Sometimes I take back my love. When I do give all of my love it is often laced with sadness and tears and pain.

But oh, what I get in return for my love is greater than anything I will ever get from hanging on to it. The Lord my God fulfills every need. He gives me new desires, new dreams, new strengths. He offers hope and peace that will never be found without Him.

The greatest commandment is this, and to it Lord, I say yes.

Thought for the Day:

Do you ever think about what it really means to love? Love can be fickle, and hard. Remember that God IS love, and He truly offers the best love of all.

From God's Word

> Jesus replied: "Love the Lord your God with all your heart and with all your soul and with all your mind." This is the first and greatest commandment. And the second is like it: "Love your neighbor as yourself." (Matthew 22:37–39, NIV)

Prayer for Today

Lord, you tell us to love you first and most, with everything in us, and then to love others. Sometimes I have trouble with love at all. Thank you for being love, that I may find my example of how to love in you. Help me grow into someone who knows how to love at all times, even when it is hard. In your holy name. Amen.

Knees in the Gramble

Lia and I went to the store one day, I with Eli in the stroller and she on her bike. She recently learned how to ride with no training wheels and is becoming quite adept at it. She followed my instructions and stopped at each intersection to walk across each road with me by her side. She rode ahead here and there, but never got too far from me. Just far enough that she could still see me, hear my voice, and listen for instruction.

Until we got closer to home.

She asked if she could ride on across the street into the driveway. I told her she could cross, but maybe she should just walk her bike up the driveway. Our driveway is a fairly steep hill of new gravel. It is loose and not the kind of thing a new bike rider should take.

Sure enough, she and the bike tipped over and she scraped up her knees. I went and picked her up, and wiped her tears. I gave her a hug and told her it would be okay, but maybe she should listen to me more closely.

Discussing it later, she talked about how she was really good at riding her bike, but probably shouldn't ride her bike in the "gramble" lest she could scrape up her knees again. I agreed.

Lia's mishap with her bike is so much like me in my own life. I will be riding along, balancing oh so well, enjoying the breeze and the scenery. I will keep Jesus just close enough that I can still hear Him and listen for His instruction. Things will go so well until I get too far ahead. I decide that I can do it without Him. I think I can take the steep road with the loose gravel and I'll be just fine. After all, I've done so well on my own so far.

But I never really was on my own. I did so well because I had His instruction. When I stop listening, it never fails—I fall down into the loose gravel and get all bruised.

Thank heavens God is such a loving parent. He will calmly come and pick me up, wipe away my tears and gently remind me that he knows best. Listen to me. I love you. Let's try this again, but this time, let me lead.

Thought for the Day

How often do you tend to be listening to God with all things going well for you, only to get too far ahead and fall flat on your face? Remember that if you stick with Him, and listen to instruction, you can't fail.

From God's Word

> The Lord upholds all who fall and lifts up all who
> are bowed down. (Psalm 145:14, NIV)

Prayer for Today

God, I know that when I listen to you and do as you say that I will be safe in your arms. Sometimes, I forget this and move ahead too fast, ignoring your voice. Help me to always remember who holds me, and that you've got my life in your hands. In Jesus' name. Amen.

Remember the Thorns

Yesterday, I was nearly giddy with excitement about the path I felt God was taking me on. I could hardly contain myself. Big things were coming my way! Yesterday, I was hopeful. Yesterday, I was on top of the world. Yesterday, I felt God was speaking directly to me.

Yesterday.

But today, not so much. Today, I am sad. Today, I don't see the big things.. Today, I don't hear God. My mood is like the weather outside—rainy, gray. My responsibilities are overwhelming, and I'm not sure I have it in me to continue.

When I feel this way, I could crawl into bed like I want to. But then, where is my hope? How can I bring joy—or hope, or the message of peace—to others when I refuse to look for it myself?

So I remembered some words from the Psalms. Actually, I remembered a specific word. *Remember.* So I looked it up and what I found was helpful and comforting.

I remembered. I pulled out my journal, and I found so many entries of blessing. There were lots of days I did not feel God near me. But there were so many days when He was right there.

When my thoughts traveled to doubt about my calling, because of my moods and such, I also remembered thorns. The apostle Paul was given a "thorn in the flesh." The Bible doesn't speak about what it was exactly, but Paul asked God three times to take it away. God refused. He said, "My grace is sufficient for you, for my power is made perfect in weakness."

So I remembered hope. I remembered peace. I remembered the power in my thorns. God's grace is sufficient for me. When I am weak, He is strong. And He will use me in whatever way He chooses.

And I'm okay with that.

Thought for the Day

Do you ever have those days that you just don't feel like you can make it through, and you wonder where God is? What do you do when that happens? Try to write down the good things that God does for you in a journal, so on the tough days, you can go back and remember all of the good that comes from the tough places.

From God's Word

> I will remember the deeds of the Lord; yes, I will remember your miracles of long ago. (Psalm 77:11, NIV)

> Remember the wonders he has done, his miracles and the judgments he pronounced. (Psalm 105:5, NIV)

Prayer for Today

Father, sometimes, I just feel like I can't do it. I want to give up and lay in bed and just quit. But then I think back on all the times you brought me through. Help me to always remember everything you have done for me. Thank you for your goodness and grace. In Jesus' name. Amen.

Distraction

The baby is in *that* stage right now. It is so much fun to watch him learn, but I am constantly having to pick him up from wherever he is and move him to a place I want him to be. He will stay for a minute, then go back to whatever exciting new thing catches his eye. He is going full force all the time from one thing to another. He has to check it all out, stick it all in his mouth, bang on it, then move on.

He is having a blast, while I am having to pick him up, move him back, pick him up, move him back, pick him up…you get the idea.

Something occurred to me tonight during my attempted quiet time. I was reading my lesson and trying to pray. I was quite unsuccessful. I kept catching myself listening to the TV in the other room. Then I'd catch myself thinking about all of the things I needed to get done. Then about all of the things I may have forgotten that I needed to get done. So many distractions!

It suddenly struck me as funny, the irony of the situation. I am in this exciting new stage of life, and trying to learn my calling. Kids are growing, my career is changing, life is different. I have these huge goals that are coming out of nowhere and I can seem to do everything but sit and speak, or more importantly, listen to God to really see where He is leading me. Too many exciting things catch my eye.

I think I'm having a blast when God picks me up and moves me back, picks me up and moves me back, picks me up…you get the idea.

Hopefully, I will grow out of this stage before the precious baby does.

Thought for the Day

When you are trying to pray, do you often find yourself getting distracted? Do you fall into the same category as your little ones in your relationship towards God? Remember that we are His children, and He will pick us up and pull us back when necessary.

From God's Word

> Therefore, holy brothers and sisters, who share in the heavenly calling, fix your thoughts on Jesus, whom we acknowledge as our apostle and high priest. (Hebrews 3:1, NIV)

Prayer for Today

Lord, just like it is easy for babies and small children, it is easy for me too to get distracted. Help me fix my thoughts on you, whatever may be going on around me. When I do stray, thank you for picking me up and putting me back where I belong. In your precious name. Amen.

But Lord

"**B**ut, Mom…"

Sweet Lia's favorite words. When Lia is told to do something, she will question it nine times out of ten.

Not to say that Lia is naughty, or even disobedient. She generally listens to you. But first she needs to know why. She calculates what she believes to be the most obvious thing that should be done at any given moment, and if you ask her to do something else, "but" is the first word she responds with.

Even though Lia's "buts" can really stretch my patience thin, I know that she loves me and her dad very much. She wants to please us. She is just inquisitive and wants to learn what's behind my reasoning. I really do love that about her, and I know that God created her that way for a reason. She is smart and focused. Her personality will serve her well when she's grown.

I was reading in the book of John tonight, and I came across the story of Mary and Martha when their brother Lazarus had died. For four days, he had been in the tomb before Jesus came to them. Jesus told them to roll away the stone from the tomb, and Martha, who seems to me a conscientious, focused gal, said, "But, Lord…"

This stuck out big time.

It led me to look up others in the Bible who were asked by God to do something and first answered with "but" before listening to his commands.

> Moses, when told to go to the Pharoah in the book of Exodus
>
> Gideon, when told to lead Israel against the Midianites in the book of Judges
>
> Jonah, when told to go to Ninevah in the book of Jonah
>
> Jeremiah, when told to speak God's words to the people in the book of Jeremiah

I'm sure this is only the beginning.

I am certainly among those who, when spoken to by my Lord, answer, "But, Lord…"

Funny how we people can be. The Lord God speaks to us and we have to speak our case first. "I don't speak well," "They don't deserve it," "I am too weak," "I am too young," and so on.

What would happen if when God spoke, we simply obeyed? I know that if Lia simply obeyed, life could be easier (albeit more boring). However, unlike me with Lia, God is *always* right. When he commands, he will always see me through. His ways are always the right way and there should never be a reason to question.

Thought for the Day

Do you have a child that likes to say "But, Mom?" How do you deal with that? How do you think God likes it when we do the same to Him? Try to remember next time He asks you to do something that He is always right, and it is best to just listen.

From God's Word

> "Take away the stone," he said.
>
> "But, Lord," said Martha, the sister of the dead man, "by this time there is a bad odor, for he has been there four days."
>
> Then Jesus said, "Did I not tell you that if you believed, you would see the glory of God?" (John 11:39–40, NIV)

Prayer for Today

Lord, I praise you for your wondrous patience. You always give me a chance to obey when I tend to first answer with a "but." May I model that patience with my children and show them love, and may I teach them to listen and obey when you speak. In your name I pray. Amen.

Breakfast in Bed

This morning, I woke up to a delicious breakfast in bed. Ava cooked me a ham, egg and cheese sandwich. She loves the fact that this is one thing that we recently taught her how to cook, and she does it as often as she is able.

As soon as I was done eating breakfast from Ava, and praised her awesome talents, Lia decided she needed to make me breakfast as well. With Ava's help, Lia made me another breakfast of eggs with lots of extra salt and pepper, and toast with peanut butter and jelly. She even brought me a glass of milk.

I love it when they decide to do these things for me. It shows that they love me and that they want to please me. I have to admit though, it makes me feel a little sheepish. I almost never make my kids a hot breakfast. Our mornings are so rushed. They are lucky to get a full bowl of cereal. On lazy weekends, since I'm confessing anyway, I even let them have ice cream for breakfast once in a while. (It has dairy, right?)

Whatever the case, it also made me wonder; What am I doing so right to make these kids love me so much? And what am I doing to please my Heavenly Father, who does far more for me than what I do for my kids? My delicious breakfasts were a great reminder for me of so many things, but the most important were these:

First, I must be a pretty good mom after all.

Second, my kids are pretty great.

And third, I have some work to do to show my Father what an awesome parent He is.

Thought for the Day

What kinds of things do your kids do to remind you that you are a good mom, and also that they are great kids? Do you do anything special to show God what a good parent He is? Think of some things you can do as a family to show your love to each other and to God.

From God's Word:

> God is not unjust; he will not forget your work and the love you have shown him as you have helped his people and continue to help them. (Hebrews 6:10, NIV)

Prayer for Today

Father, thank you for being such a good parent to me. Show me how I can show my love for you. Thank you for my children and the blessings they bring. Help me do my best to parent them by following your guidance. In Jesus' name. Amen.

Joy in the Jumble

Note: I wrote this during one of the first few weeks of my third baby's life. It means so much to me, and I thought it might say something to you as well, so I've included it so you know that if you are in this stage, you are not alone.

My thoughts are jumbled. My eyes are half shut. Should probably be in bed, but so much to do. Just put the baby down, need some mom time. I am wet with baby puke. I am hungry. Better not eat, I have too much weight to lose. The house is a disaster. The bed needs to be made so I can crawl in…but wait, there is a new show I want to watch. Will I even remember it? There's laundry to be done. Am I forgetting something? Most likely. I usually am. Thank goodness I have tomorrow off from work. But still so much to do. Back to full time soon. Will I survive?

Of course. Stressed, but I always make it out alive. Don't panic! I really need to get more organized…Or hire a housekeeper. I'm spiraling into a sea of negativity.

But wait, what's that? A song coming from my son's bedroom grabs my attention. "Jesu, Joy of Man's Desiring" in calliope like music. It is putting him to sleep. It's making me smile. I have so much to be grateful for. I was trying to pray. God was trying to talk. He is here. He has given me instructions on how to have joy in all. Clear as day if only I listen and obey. He has opened His arms to provide rest and comfort. And all I had to do was seek Him. Listen for Him. Hear Him. Now can I keep it up? Can I drown out the callings and resist the pull to work and worry, just for a second? Of course. I have a good leader. I may fall, but I will get back up. I will hold my thoughts captive to Christ. And I will find joy in the jumble.

Will you?

Thought for the Day

Have you ever been here? Overwhelmed with all the work that must be done? Take time to listen to what God may have to say to you amidst the jumble in your life.

From God's Word

> Do not be anxious about anything, but in every situation, by prayer and petition, with thanksgiving, present your requests to God. And the peace of God, which transcends all understanding, will guard your hearts and your minds in Christ Jesus. (Philippians 4:6–7, TNIV)

Prayer for Today

Lord, sometimes my life feels like a big jumble of things to do, little people to care for, and messes to clean up. Help me place all of my cares on you, and fill my heart and my mind with your peace. Thank you for this promise you give. In Jesus' name. Amen.

Give Thanks

In the hustle and bustle of our busy lives, it can be so easy to get in a funk. In these frigid Minnesota winters—with a lack of sunshine—it's pretty easy to fall into a habit of complaining and seeing the yuck. When life gets tough, I tend to forget just how important it is to think about the good and thank the One who gives it.

This past week has been kind of a tough one for my family. We had an unexpected death, another family member has to move from the home she knows and is struggling with other issues, some of us have been fighting illness and pain, and the stress on others has been overwhelming. These are the times you kind of feel like throwing in the towel.

But when I put my focus on the good, I can see how God is working through it all. The funeral we attended was wonderful and time with family precious. We had shared wonderful memories together. Our ride home was treacherous in the weather, but we safely arrived back to Sweet Home Sweet (Lia's words). I believe our other dear family member has found a wonderful new home that will suit her needs well. Illnesses and pain are improving. We have weathered the storms and I believe it has offered us a learning experience for future challenges.

It is so easy to complain to others of all the bad that we face, and in this fallen world there is a lot of it. But sometimes, we need to spread the word about the good we have amidst it all. When we give thanks and spread the good news of what He has done, we can offer hope to those in their own trials. I pray that you can see the good in your bad times and make known to the nations what He has done for you. May your thankfulness spread to those in need.

Thought for the Day

Do you often have a hard time seeing the good when times are tough? What can you do with your family to make it a little easier? Don't forget, count your blessings and you'll be surprised at the good it can bring!

From God's Word

> Finally, brothers and sisters, whatever is true, whatever is noble, whatever is right, whatever is pure, whatever is lovely, whatever is admirable—if anything is excellent or praiseworthy—think about such things. (Philippians 4:8, NIV)

Prayer for Today

Lord, sometimes it is so easy to get down in the dumps when things aren't going my way. When this happens, it seems to be catchy to those around me, including my children. Please help me remember all of the good things you have done, and think of that alone to get me through. Thank you for your blessings on me. In your holy name. Amen.

Doing Dishes in Heaven

My sweet Lia hit me with a big one today.

"Mom, I am going to be dead by tomorrow."

Uffda.

My first reaction was to swallow the lump in my throat, grab her tight, tell her never to say such a thing again, and never let her go.

However, that is not how to deal with Miss Lia. She likes to hit you with these crazy things, and the best thing to do is nonchalantly answer her with just as much normalcy as you can muster.

So I took a breath and I simply said, "No, you're not."

"Yes, I am."

"Well, I hope not. I will really miss you."

"Why? I'll see you in heaven. We will play and you will do the dishes."

Hmmm. I replied, "I hope I don't have to do dishes in heaven. I don't really like doing dishes."

And that was the end of the conversation. What a character. She certainly makes me think. How wonderful that my kid is totally cool with the fact that she's going to heaven when she's done here on earth. She knows it's a good place to be. I sincerely hope it's a long time before we see each other there. However, I know that whatever may happen, God has us both in the palm of His hand and we have nothing to fear.

Oh, and if I do have to do dishes in heaven, I will do them joyfully.

Thought for the Day

Have any of your kids ever said anything to you that made you cringe? Or something that made you think deeply about your place in life? Think of how you may answer them, or what you can learn from your children in these instances.

From God's Word

> If I go up to the heavens, you are there; if I make my bed in the depths, you are there. (Psalm 139:8, NIV)

Prayer for Today

Our Father in heaven, thank you for the wonderful place you have made for us to live with you when we leave this earth. For sending your Son to die for us so that if we believe in Him, we shall live forever with you in heaven. You are so good. Give me and my children the confidence to know that if we believe in you, we will see you face to face someday, and even if dishes are required, it will be a joyful place to be. In your name. Amen.

My BFF

I was incredibly pregnant, incredibly emotional, and incredibly impatient. I wanted to go to a Lenten church service with my family. My husband just wanted to go home. He was tired and ready for some R & R. He was being thoughtful and decided to stay at church with me anyway.

However, almost the whole church service was spent on his smart phone. I was livid.

My emotions got the best of me, and rather than enjoy the service myself, I became overwhelmed with anger toward my hubby.

After the service, I stormed out in tears.

My friend quickly noticed what was going on and asked my husband what the matter was.

"Hormones," he replied.

Oooohhh, nothing like that response to make an angry pregnant woman even angrier.

I hung back with my angry tears while my hubby took the kiddos to the car. My friend walked alongside me and asked, "Okay, what's *really* going on? You know you can tell me the truth."

And tell her I did. I let it all out, and she listened intently. She then gave me a hug and sent me on my way. She never made a bad remark about my husband to make things worse, but supported me in my overwhelmed emotions and gave me her full attention as a friend.

The next day at work, I received a little gift package. It contained my most favorite things—a chocolate bar, an orange pop, and a beautiful journal. It also came with a card and a note. While reading the encouraging, honest note, I came to the realization that for the first time in my adult life, I had a real, tried and true best girlfriend, and someone that could understand me like my best husband friend could not. I had received a blessing like no other.

(PS, my hubby and I were just fine too!)

Thought for the Day

Do you have any close women friends to talk to? If not, think about joining a women's group of some sort to make some new friends. Most importantly, remember, being a good friend is just as important as having one!

From God's Word

> Perfume and incense bring joy to the heart, and the pleasantness of a friend springs from their heartfelt advice. (Proverbs 27:9, NIV)

Prayer for Today

Lord Jesus, thank you for my friends. Thank you for blessing us with those people in our lives who know us exactly for who we are and love us anyway. Thank you for giving us those people with whom we can be our true selves. In your name. Amen.

Nap Time

I've been burning the candle at both ends lately.

With the baby's (non) schedule, the girls' activities, work, and regular daily life, I haven't exactly been getting the sleep I need.

I always feel the push to get everything done. The house has to be clean (it never is), the laundry should be washed, folded and put away (that's never going to happen), not to mention I like to take time for my writing (which I'm doing right now—smiles!).

I'm not complaining. I have the help of my fabulous husband, and the girls are old enough to do chores, but it just seems like a never-ending cycle of doing until we drop.

This afternoon, I was feeling especially run down. So when I came home on my lunch break, I laid down for just a second. And woke up a half an hour later. Good thing I'd set my alarm just in case. The kitty and I had a great nap.

I felt fantastic.

It made me think. Who says the house has to be clean all the time? Who says the laundry must be one hundred percent done? Who says that we have to constantly be running around like mad people? I really don't think we are being judged on these things by anyone but ourselves. They will still be there tomorrow. And the next day. And unfortunately the day after that.

Sometimes, we just need to take time to smell the roses. To spend extra time with our family and friends. To rest and relax. Even God rested after six days of hard work, which is why He created the Sabbath as a day of rest for us.

Sometimes, we need to take note about what God's Word says about rest, and see that even the baby knows just what to do.

Take a nap.

Thought for the Day

Do you find yourself neglecting the important rest time that God has created for us? Rest is good for you, and necessary to keep on going in life. Be still, and know God is God, and the rest is good.

From God's Word

> Then God blessed the seventh day and made it holy, because on it he rested from all the work of creating that he had done. (Genesis 2:3, NIV)

Prayer for Today

Lord, it can be so very hard for me to take the time to get the rest and nurturing sleep that my body needs. I know that it is important, but it seems there is so much to get done. Thank you for creating the Sabbath for us, as a reminder that rest is important, and holy, and good. Help me to use that time to come to you and receive refreshment. In Jesus' holy name. Amen.

Encouragement and Pixie Hollow

My poor Lia has an ear infection. Still. Again. She hasn't totally been herself for a while now. Her eyes aren't quite as bright as usual, and she needs to have more medicine. She complains of a headache. I just want to snuggle her up.

Through all of this though, she keeps a good attitude. She doesn't think of the bad. She thinks about nice things. On the way home from the doctor tonight, she asked me in all seriousness when she could go and visit Pixie Hollow. I told her she probably couldn't because Pixie Hollow is not on Earth. "I know," she said, "but I can still go." I asked her how she was going to get there. "I'll just follow the star!" Simple as that. This kid just knows how it is. She knows what she wants to do and how she's going to do it.

She encourages me every day. Just by being her.

I was talking about my year-long goals the other day and my sweet Ava piped up. She wants to be part of my group of encouragers. She is going to help me.

I got flowers from my fabulous husband yesterday, along with a wonderful note of encouragement.

The Lord has blessed me with such a wonderful group of friends and family. If I pay attention and look around, in all the mess that I deal with on a daily basis, I am still surrounded by encouragement. Sometimes, I just need to be open to it and watchful of it. I only hope that I can follow the example of those around me and remember to encourage others. Together, along with Jesus, we can move mountains.

Thought for the Day

When was the last time someone encouraged you in something? What can you do to encourage your spouse, or your children? Think of something you can do today to bring encouragement to another. They will reap the benefits, and so will you!

From God's Word

> Your love has given me great joy and encouragement, because you, brother, have refreshed the hearts of the Lord's people. (Philemon 1:7, NIV)

Prayer for Today

Lord, when I read your Word, you bring encouragement to me. Thank you for the many people you have surrounded me with that bring encouragement to me also. Help me encourage others in return. In Jesus' name. Amen.

Of Babies and Missing Brain Cells

For me, my sweet baby number one was a breeze. I always remembered what I needed and felt like I had it together as a mom. After my second daughter was born however, my brain was not quite the same as it had been before. I think when I gave birth to her I lost a few brain cells. I quickly learned that life would not be as easy as it had previously been.

My first real outing with the two of them together was to my in-laws. I bundled up my toddler and the precious new babe for protection against the winter air. I strapped them into the car safely and did a quick double check on everything before the short drive into town.

As babies often do, my new little baby needed a diaper change as soon as we reached our destination. It only took a second for me to realize we had a problem.

I had forgotten the diaper bag.

I did not react well to the realization that I had forgotten such an important accessory that all babies require—diapers. I quickly dissolved into a frustrated, blubbering mess. What a failure.

My mother-in-law was quick to remind me that this was not a life or death situation, and she watched the kiddos while I ran to the store for the much needed diapers. The day was saved.

I now have three precious children and often think back on this and smile. If only I knew then what I know now. Forgotten diapers? Ha, that's nothing. Just wait until you forget to strap them into the carseat.

Thought for the Day

Have you ever felt like a failure because you have forgotten something important for your children, or yourself? Do you think of turning to God when this happens? The next time you feel down on yourself due to your lack of perfection, practice praying for the peace that you need.

From God's Word

> You will keep in perfect peace those whose minds are steadfast, because they trust in you. (Isaiah 26:3, NIV)

Prayer for Today

Thank you, Lord, that you can offer me peace through all of the trials that motherhood brings. If only I keep my trust in you and you alone, I can have complete peace knowing that all things turn out according to your will. Give me the peace I so desire in you, and the wisdom to know that you are in control, whether I bring the diaper bag or not. In the precious name of Jesus. Amen.

Finding My Worth
in the Checkout Line

I'm standing in line at the grocery store and staring at me from the cover of a magazine is a picture of a very famous, very beautiful pop star. She was showing off her world—meaning the only parts of her that were covered were—well, you get the picture.

Part of me was disgusted and frustrated. This woman is a role model, whether she likes it or not. The picture was inappropriate and should not be sitting out in the open for all the world to see. How can I teach my girls that real beauty comes from your heart and not your body? How can I expect them to respect themselves and have modesty when nakedness surrounds them? How can I teach my boy to practice purity when his eyes will be bombarded with pictures like this?

Another part of me felt like rushing home, waxing my lady mustache and buying a girdle. I felt unworthy. My emotions rush back to junior high and high school when my self-esteem was based on my comparison to other girls.

I don't add up. Never did. Probably never will. My body was not made like this woman's. I naturally went to comparing myself to her, and all the other stars pasted on the covers of those magazines. The only ones I might compare to are the "guess who's cellulite this is" pictures in the tabloids.

Then my daughter pipes up. "She should put some clothes on! It's not nice to be looking like that."

I smiled. "I agree! She sure would look better with clothes on."

I remembered that my worth comes not at all from my looks, but from my Savior. He is enthralled by my beauty (and lucky for me, so is my hubby!) So far, my daughters seem to be learning this truth too, so I think their daddy and I are doing something right. I guess I just need to keep doing what I'm doing, so my kids learn respect for themselves and others. I want them to know their true worth—worth that comes from being truly loved by God.

Thought for the Day

Do you find the way women are flaunting themselves off-putting? Do you find yourself sometimes wishing you looked the way that they did? Do you place your self-esteem in your looks? Try considering this: Self-esteem is of no worth. God-esteem, on the other hand, is worth everything.

From God's Word

> Your beauty should not come from outward adornment, such as elaborate hairstyles and the wearing of gold jewelry or fine clothes. Rather, it should be that of your inner self, the unfading beauty of a gentle and quiet spirit, which is of great worth in God's sight. (1 Peter 3:3–4, NIV)

Prayer for Today

Lord God, thank you for giving me God-esteem. For showing me that I am worthy of your love and the love of others because of your Son. Help me remember that my beauty truly is in my relationship with you. In your precious name. Amen.